UTAH
Gateway to Nevada!

UTAH Gateway to Nevada!

A SPECIAL NOTE TO THE VISITOR:

You anxiously scan the pages of your Rand McNally on the seat beside you. Desperate computations and alternative routes are carefully considered before the awful reality sets in: the fastest way to get from Colorado to Nevada takes you through terra igcognita-- Utah; and like a modern day Magellan, through Utah you must go.

Literally dozens of ill-advised and ill-fated travelers yearly reach this inescapable conclusion. It is to these intrepid realists that we dedicate this book. For the Beehive State is more than 300 miles of chuckholed blacktop linking the Colorado and Wyoming Rockies to neon-splattered gambling meccas of eastern Nevada; Utah is much more than a funny shaped buffer that keeps Idaho's mountains and lakes from falling into the Grand Canyon. The many cornered state has a higher purpose than simply providing a spot where tourists can stand in Utah, New Mexico, Colorado and Arizona at the same time; but nobody knows what it is.

Like Dante's "inferno" wherein the nether regions of Hades are laid bare and opened to the wayward tourist, Gateway editors have striven to make your short visit to this neat state as comprehensible and bearable as possible. So whether you're merely traveling non-stop from east to west, or veering south off the inter-state on a dare or because you lost a bet, you'll appreciate a copy of Utah: Gateway to Nevada! tucked safely in your jockey box. Find out firsthand that Utah is not just the sum of her many varied and unique corners. You'll come away (if you do indeed get away) a far more enlightened motorist than when you stumbled in, secure in your knowledge that Utah is truly and unavoidably the Gateway to Nevada.

UTAH
Gateway to Nevada!

Tim Kelly
Neil Passey
Mark Knudsen

Dream Garden Press
Salt Lake City
1984

A lot of people have generously offered their support, suggestions or an occasional round of beer. We would like to thank Cathy, Sharon, Max, Ause, Redeye, Kristen, Brad, Kerry, Rebecca, Ollie, Patrick and Paul, Pat, Bob and Jean, Charley, Morrie and Helen, Doug and Bruce at the Trophy Shop, Ken, Marc, Paul, Lynn, Denny and Heather—to name a few.

Con Psarras' insightful editing and comments on the text were a great help.

Finally, a special note of gratitude to our typist, Orin Hatch, for unflagging patience and a consistently cheery smile throughout what was surely a demeaning and dirty little chore.

The contents of this book are fictional and meant to be taken with an oversized grain of salt. Any resemblance to persons past or present is coincidental.

Utah — The Incredible State

Copyright © 1984 by Dream Garden Press.

Manufactured in the United States of America.

Library of Congress Number: 84-071463
ISBN: 0-942688-05-8

C   D

Dream Garden Press • 1199 Iola Avenue
Salt Lake City, Utah 84104

Prologue

To the Indians she was known as WEZ-TUH-VAL-EE-SIH-TEE, which means *"bird that honks when provoked."* And her grandeur and promise was theirs.

Later, Mormon settlers pushed west and made her their mountain home. They named her "Utah," after Gordy Utah, the revered frontier hairdresser, the man who tamed the split ends of the West, the creator of the beehive hairdo. We remember.

Our long vigil of sacrifice links yesteryear with today and has given birth to a society that is capable of facing the challenge of the future with a vacant grin.

From all five corners of this neat state, from the big mountains to the flat salt flats, from the nice valleys to the dry deserts, we proclaim: *"Flip yes, we're from Utah!"*

The abandoned pre-Anazani refrigerator in the foreground
indicates that Father Escalante made it as far north as Kearns.

The Legend

History, Legend, Lore, Reverence

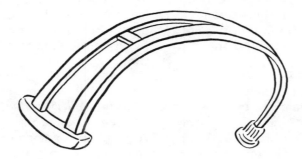

Econۤᴏᴍɪsт Joseph Alois Schumpeter once remarked,
"...history sometimes indulges in jokes of questionable
taste." In the same vein, R.V. sales specialist Boyd Bigler once
remarked, "...the development of Utah is to history as the fart
joke is to humor."

Although Dr. Schumpeter probably had a point, we feel that
Boyd was just trying to get a cheap laugh. Even if one takes into
account the fact that the geographical boundaries of the
proposed state of Deseret bore a remarkable resemblance to a
whoopie cushion, *Gateway* editors are unanimous in denouncing
Mr. Bigler's assertion as vulgar and inaccurate.

We feel that the history of this great state is more properly
compared to a rubber crutch joke.

The Legend

History, Legend, Lore, Reverence

Prehistory

THE dawn of human settlement in the region now known as Utah echoes through the ages, preserved as rock paintings, obscure and frequently off-color Indian legends, and abandoned Indian dwellings.

Though the relics that survive are limited, in the capable hands of a scientific investigator a coherent tale can be reconstructed. The thorny question of how the Indians got here in the first place is answered by the Book of Mormon in one way and by science in another. Setting that controversy aside for individual discrimination, our tale begins at an archeological dig fifteen miles southwest of the modern community of No Gas.

There, amid the abandoned Chevys, the oldest known remains of an Indian village in Utah have been uncovered by Dr. Barry Huffacre and his team of archeologists. Their work has given us a sketchy idea of the daily life of these early peoples.

Dr. Huffacre describes an unearthed stone coa coa table. Found with the table were an artful bunch of pre nic-nac puma bone grapes and a petroglyphic depiction of three braves holding curious cone shaped objects. In addition, two suggestive finds— the fragments of a primitive hand-produced polyester, plus pictographs tentatively deciphered as, "We love Uncle Peterson,"— led him to the formulation of the Theory of the Proto Mormon, in which he suggests that ingestion of the indigenous wild miniature marshmallow (*Unrulus mallow smallus*) effects a change in certain amino acids in the cerebral cortex resulting in specific behavioral changes.

Dr. Huffacre goes on to outline the substantial evidence suggesting that the Proto Mormons sent pairs of young braves (claiming to be Jewish and denouncing the use of the peace pipe) on forays into neighboring regions.

Indian legend passed on as oral tradition from that bygone era to this bygone era tells us: "Spider spun the earth and the sky, but is in no way responsible for the full length puff sleeve dress."

Exploration

An assortment of mountain men, trappers and prospectors comprised the vanguard of the white man's incursion into the Utah area. But the first Caucasian to get hopelessly lost in the region was Father Valez de Escalante. (See pages 6 and 20.)

Another hero of the early days, Gordy Utah, was a man whose career spanned the era of exploration and the time of settlement by the Mormon pioneers. Known as the hairdresser of the western frontier, the man who tamed the split ends of the West, and the namesake of our great state, Gordy had extraordinary vision and courage.

He established "Salon d'Utah" on the location that is presently occupied by "Zion's A-1 Cyclery" at a time when most of his visitors were lizards. He created the beehive hairdo at a time  when the average set- tler was still wearing braids and bonnets.

Col. Jim Bridger traversed the Salt Lake Valley frequently, and each time left hating it a little more. Nevertheless, it was his custom to stop by "Salon d'Utah" for a moustache trim and a body perm.

Brigham Young's hit man, Porter Rockwell, once stabbed Gordy in the knee for back combing. Braving the pain, through clenched jaws, Gordy Utah spoke those famous words, "Leave this instant, you beast."

Such was the hardship of the early days of frontier cosmetology.

Settlement

From New York to Nauvoo, and on to Council Bluffs and Winter Quarters on the Missouri, to Ft. Kearny, Ft. Laramie, Ft. Bridger and across the Rockies, they marched. They came in the wake of persecution, hounded by their neighbors, dogged by the Federal Government.

They moved onward, pushing their carts ahead of them toward the bleak promise of a forbidding land.

There is an old pioneer story that tells how only one tree was visible in the Salt Lake Valley when Mormon settlers arrived at the mouth of Emigration Canyon. The story is true. The tree was a potted palm, and its owner was Gordy Utah. Later he was to tell Brigham Young, "I had just set it outside for a day or two while the decorators were here."

After much hardship, the settlers arrived and planted crops in hopes of a late harvest.

They built shelters and prepared for winter.

Then disaster struck. First one, then two, then several hundred million crickets descended on the ripening wheat fields.

What was needed was a miracle, and some say that "miracle" is the only word to describe what happened next. (For detailed discussion see page 16.)

A search through journals of the original settlers for accounts of the miraculous nature of this much-discussed incident turned up a number of interesting passages, but none more telling than the entry from the diary of Kimball Bigler: "What with the crickets eating everything in sight and those damned beagle doo-dahs you step in when you're not looking, not to mention tripping over lawyers every time I turn around, it's a miracle if a man can get any time at all to see his hairdresser."

Although the first winter was hard and lean, the pioneers survived and began to prosper. Two years after their arrival the gold rush to California started, and trade with the '49ers made many of the faithful richer than most of those who pushed on to the Pacific.

Now let's consider the distinctions between legend and history. Also, what distinguishes these two from lore?

History and legend both deal with events in the past. The difference is mainly a matter of style and credentials. In Utah especially, the boundaries that divide them are soft, out of focus, sometimes completely inverted. And we applaud this. You're not going to catch *Gateway* editors giving facts a bloated and unnecessary emphasis. Which leads us to lore. Everyone has heard the phrase, "He's steeped in scout lore," or something similar. One never "gets steeped" in history or legend, only in lore of one kind or another. So it can be said that lore is a vessel for steeping.

We're glad to have cleared that up.

Utah is rife with history and legend, and virtually bloated with lore, so let's take a stroll through the dubious chapters of a past that's begging to be forgotten.

This is the Place?—Video Tape

There is an account, widely believed and broadly disseminated concerning the single most important moment in the history of this area. It runs something like this:

Brigham Young, second Prophet of the Mormon Church and leader of a courageous band of harassed but faithful followers, embarked from Nauvoo, Illinois on a westward trek that ended after considerable hardship at the mouth of what is now called Emigration Canyon. Nearly blind with tick fever, his gaze was nevertheless clear and penetrating as he assessed the desolate valley before him. He then spoke the immortal words: "This is the place." His most trusted followers at his left and right, the flock a respectful pace or two behind, Brigham confidently led the party to their new home in the Salt Lake Valley.

Wrong. He didn't actually say that. The rest of it is pretty close, but he didn't say, "This is the place"; and we have a video tape to prove it. Here for the first time history opens its jammed doors to give us a tantalizing peek at the events of this pivotal moment as they actually occurred.

Roll 'em...

THIS IS THE PLACE?
CREDITS

Producer	Alfonzo Rae Bigler
Director	Cubby Peterson
Art Director	LaNancy Smith
Make-up	LaMindy Fay Young
Camera	ChadMar Tuttle
Boom	Boyce B. Boyce
Best Boy	L'il Josh Crawlspace
Key Grip	El Rae Dean Huffacre
Unit Production Manager	LaTandy Rae Bigler
Special Guest Star	Brigham Young

Scene: *Brigham Young and the pioneers are standing at the mouth of Emigration Canyon gazing at the arid, treeless wasteland before them.*

Pioneers: Mutter, mutter, mutter.

Brigham Young: This is the pits.

THE END

The Mormon Trail

The trail blazed by the Mormon pioneers in their exodus west and the hardships suffered along it constitute one of the great chapters in American history. Key events in the trek are noted in the accompanying map.

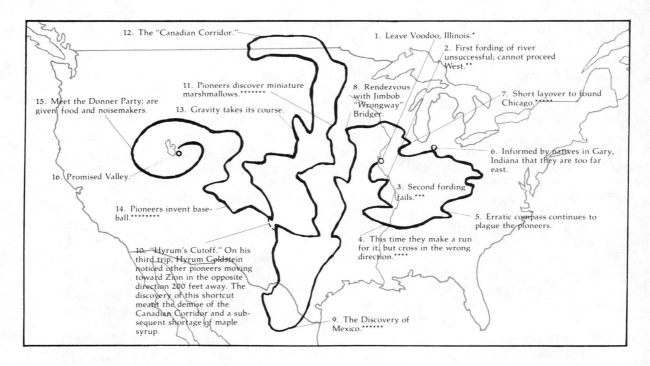

12. The "Canadian Corridor."

1. Leave Voodoo, Illinois.*

2. First fording of river unsuccessful; cannot proceed West.**

11. Pioneers discover miniature marshmallows.*******

8. Rendezvous with Jimbob "Wrongway" Bridger.

7. Short layover to found Chicago.*****

15. Meet the Donner Party; are given food and noisemakers.

13. Gravity takes its course.

6. Informed by natives in Gary, Indiana that they are too far east.

16. Promised Valley.

3. Second fording fails.***

14. Pioneers invent baseball.********

5. Erratic compass continues to plague the pioneers.

10. "Hyrum's Cutoff." On his third trip, Hyrum Goldstein noticed other pioneers moving toward Zion in the opposite direction 200 feet away. The discovery of this shortcut meant the demise of the Canadian Corridor and a subsequent shortage of maple syrup.

4. This time they make a run for it, but cross in the wrong direction.****

9. The Discovery of Mexico.******

*Brigham's wife Maxine bears him a son.

**First attempt to ford Mississippi fails because of "craven images on passing paddlewheel steamers."

***Second attempt to ford also fails, due to Mark Twain calling out "vast and profane proclamations."

****Brigham's wife Barbi bears him a daughter.

*****Brigham's wife Jewel bears him twin boys.

******Brigham's wife Phyllis bears him a daughter.

*******Brigham's wife Toni bears him another daughter.

********His wife Judy bears him a son.

The Handcart Pioneers

The journey is over. Pioneer settlers gaze with satisfaction into the promised valley.
Later, an intrepid party will return the Saints' handcarts.

Brigham Meets Gordy

The memorable first encounter between the two indomitable giants of early Utah history was marked by predictable conflict. Brigham Young, second prophet, seer, and revelator of the Mormon Church, first met frontier hairdresser Gordy Utah (the man with the fastest curling iron in the West) on a Wednesday.

LaGidget Young — Anoint My What?

A medium gray page from the annals of Mormon history, the suppressed saga of La Gidget Young, twenty-eighth wife of prophet Brigham Young and one of only a handful of female mule-skinners, has at long last come to light.

A researcher for *Gateway* discovered the Gidget Diaries cleverly hidden beneath the basketball equipment in the cellar under the chapel at the Nosebleed Ninth Wardhouse. We recorded a representative page below.

"Wednesday, May 19 in this year of 1860 Dear Diary,

How I, La Gidget, mule-skinner and chosen fox, could ever have thought Seer Brigham a neat guy vexes this poor girlish mind.

From this perspective of two months wedlock most holy, I proclaim myself to be bounteously ignored.

The problem really began a score of years ago when Momma confided that "polygamy" was the name given to the dish prepared with cornmeal and miniature marshmallows. In general, an unwillingness to discuss certain subjects left me surprised at..."

It's well known that later in her life La Gidget went on to found the Mr. Mule-Skinner correspondence school. It is to her credit that she was able to amass a fortune while waiting in line.

La Gidget Young

Her last words before departing this world are rumored to have been, "Neat guy, my ass." *Gateway* editors are nearly unanimous in believing that she was referring to the mule she so lovingly skinned that morning before breakfast.

The Miracle of the Lawyers

The legend of the crickets is shrouded in mystery and controversy. In fact, official church documents record conflicting versions. One account has it that on the eve of the Saints' first harvest in the Salt Lake Valley, a plague of crickets descended on the ripening crops:

"And Heavenly Father did send forth a pack of beagles yapping most mightily with bounteous wagging of tails and baying, and they did righteously point. And the crickets, when they did see and hear, did henceforth depart from that land. And they were sore afraid."

Pearl of Ray Price, 1:51

Another version records that Heavenly Father sent a vast contingent of unemployed lawyers against the crickets:

"Behold, now it came to pass that the lawyers were clothed in righteousness and three-piece suits, and did gather as a multitude to contend before the crickets. And they did issue writs and did also confound them with much jargon, saying: 'And this will be a sign unto you, that you shall be cited for bounteous felonies and misdemeanors.' And the crickets did see the mighty wagging and pointing and did hear the baying. And they were thus cast out from among them without lunch."

Book of Normal 6:9

Beagle Monument

In honor of the beagle's wondrous contribution to Mormon history.
"The best darned statue of a dog since Diogenes died."—Boyd Bigler

**BEAGLE
MONUMENT**
TEMPLE SQUARE,
SALT LAKE CITY, UTAH
In the background is the
mysterious "Assembly Hall"—
the function of which is
unknown to Mormons and
non-Mormons alike.

Dreams of Empire

THE STATE OF DESERET

This map shows the original State of Deseret as proclaimed by the prophet upon settling in the region now known as Utah. This map also shows the famous "Pacific Corridor" which linked the Deseret and California territories to the Sandwich, Solomon and Society islands.

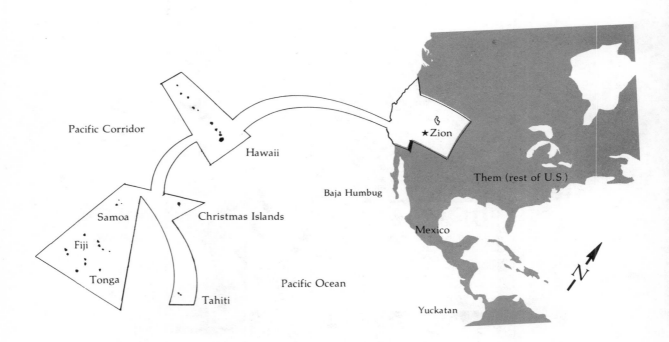

Utah Becomes a State

Although not quite the Empire Brigham Young wanted, the Utah Territory did grow impressively as it reached out to its present state boundaries.

1850. The original Territory of Utah, ceded to Deseret by an act of Congress. After the occupation of the U.S. Army.

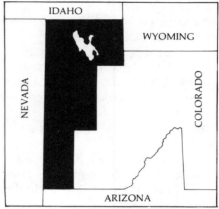

1853. Utah gains Nevada-held land. A practical joke in Nevada netted Utah six new borders. Negotiations to give the land back were futile.

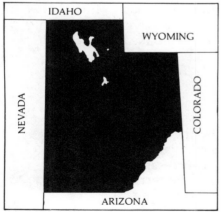

1854. The Colorado-Carson Compromise. This land, greatly enlarging our neat state, was won in a card game with the Governor of Colorado.

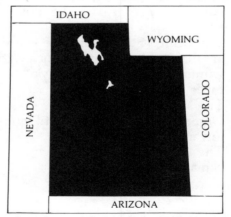

1860. Our State. This last slice of the pie was won in the famous Duck-Indian Wars. Although Utah lost, it had to keep the land.

Significant Facts in Utah History
(Distorted Beyond Recognition
For Our Own Self-Serving Purposes)

1776   Father Silvestre Valez de Escalante establishes a Motel Six and discovers the remains of a paleolithic refrigerator in the Utah region.

1777   The Indians become quite depressed.

1824   Jimbob Bridger makes a fool of himself while sinking in the Great Salt Lake.

1825   The Indians are still feeling rather despondent.

1843   Frontier hairdresser, Gordy Utah, is expelled from the region by chief Grief Eagle for coiffing Little Tree Trunk, the chief's favorite, with a salt and pepper double beehive.

1847   Brigham Young leads the first band of Mormon pioneers into the Salt Lake Valley to hear the keynote address.

1848   The United States wins the Utah area from Mexico by producing the winning Lucky Scratch 'n Match cards.

1849   The Mormons establish the state of Deseret. The Indians are still quite low about the whole thing.

1850   The Duck-Indian Wars reach a climax.

1850   Acting on the advice of Delmar "Delmar" Larsen, Congress establishes the Utah Territory.

1860   The pony express delivers its first letter in the Utah region, an overdue book notice to LeGrand Pratt from the Ft. Lauderdale Public Library.

1861   Telegraph lines meet in Salt Lake City. The first wire received is a surprisingly abusive message to LeGrand Pratt from the Ft. Lauderdale Public Library.

1869   The transcontinental railroad is finished at Promontory. The first passengers are a swat team out of Ft. Lauderdale.

1869   LeGrand Pratt returns home from the beet fields to find that 96 of his chickens have been plucked naked and his prized copy of *The Total Electric Kitchen* is missing from his shelves.

1869   A naked chicken by the name of Percy launches an unsuccessful bid for the territorial Governor's seat.

1878   Chief Grief Lizard, the grandson of Chief Grief Eagle, is quoted as saying, "I'm feeling sort of emotionally static at this point."

1890 The Mormons prohibit polygamy on the grounds that it is prohibited.

1896 Utah receives statehood. The Indians are feeling very, very depressed about the way things are developing.

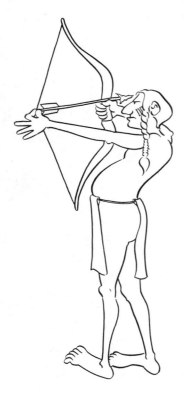

1913 The U.S. Bureau of Reclamation completes Strawberry Reservoir. Mormon scientists invent water skiing.

1915 The first airborne rats buzz Brigham City.

1924 The Indians experience random cases of burnout. Minor complaints of alienation and free floating anxiety circulate through the tribes.

1952 Uranium is discovered in southern Utah and Plutonium State Park is proposed.

1968 Social scientist, Dr. Irma Crawlspace, advises the Indians to get in touch with their feelings.

1970 The Herculom Co. establishes a financial beach head in the Spanish Fork area. Their corporate motto, "Gloriosky! It's a Herculom," angers thousands.

1971 The Indians are feeling much better as Valium replaces Wampum.

1980 The Herculom-Electralux merger threatens the economic stability of the entire region.

1982 The Indians begin to enter the mainstream middle-class culture in large numbers and learn for the first time the true meaning of the word "depression."

1987 Arabs buy the Mormon Church.

Indian Rites and Ruins

Traveling through most areas of Utah is similar to traveling backwards in time, back to an enchanted land inhabited by a mysterious people—a mysterious, albeit enchanted race of quaintly-civilized Indians known today only as the "Anazani." No one knows what these ancient people called themselves; "Anazani" is a Duck-Indian word that simply translated means "Zany Ancestors."

Whoever these enchanted people may have been, we know now that they had an advanced architecture that outlasted the subdivisions of West Valley City and that they tilled the once fertile soil of the present day Plutonium National Park, living on a simple diet of maize-dogs, lizards and native marshmallows. Aside from the structural ruins of the Anazani, who inexplicably abandoned the region in 1847, the only surviving remains of their culture are the signs and symbols they left painted and pecked into the rocks— markings that have continued to baffle archeologists to this day.

Ruins:
(as interpreted by scientists)

"Sites were frequently built in seemingly inaccessible places … this … may have been a lookout … tower or an … observatory."

"This spacious dwelling, obviously that … of a high ranking … tribesman (Falling Water) … was built over an intermittent stream …. Astronomical orientation is obvious … the foundation is … frankly laid right …."

"Multi-storied dwellings are not uncommon. This structure was oriented to the Pole-star ... calendrical significance ... is ... unavoidable ...."

Some rites of these vanished peoples have survived to this day. Many people still appear to practice the Thunda-Bird ritual of the Earthfirst and kindred tribes, which involves the ingestion of the sacred liquid, followed by a complex dance which culminates in the "shattering of the vessel

which holds the magic fluid." The ceremony begins to wind down as one by one the participants succumb to a trance-like meditation, vaguely resembling sleep. Remnants and shards of the holy vessels can be found today by pot-hunters throughout Utah, even in urban areas.

The Anazani also left writings in stone: PETROGLYPHS which are chiseled into the rock itself, and PICTOGRAPHS, created by smearing an organic gunk on the stone itself.

Pictographs/Petroglyphs: (as interpreted by noted authorities)

Commonly called the "All-American Hitch-hiker,"" ... this image is without a ... doubt a shamanistic gesture ... complete with medicine bag."

Popularly referred to as the "Saturday Nite Special,"" ... this image probably ... involved in fertility rites ...."

The famous "Sinclair" glyph. "This ... enigmatic image ... is without doubt ... an Anazani artist's attempt to picture a coyote ...."

The Driving of the Golden Spike

California Governor Leland Stanford drives the "golden spike" that links the nation together via the transcontinental railroad. The spike consists of rich milk chocolate and is covered with gleaming foil. Brigham Young was sulking in a nearby tent when this historic photo was taken but nevertheless obtained the right to market golden-spike facsimiles.

Ghost Towns—*Provo*

From its rowdy beginnings during the pig-iron rush of the 1870s, Provo showed signs of becoming a major center for steel production and higher learning.

Today, you walk its deserted streets amid an eerie silence. Perhaps a tumbleweed will rush past and catch on a rusted Rambler stationwagon or the remains of an old ward teacher, only to free itself and continue helter skelter through the loneliness, through the lost promise of Provo.

Pause to listen: the wind, only the wind whistling through the tumbledown store fronts, the fallen golden arches. Softly it seems to whisper, "Where the flip is everybody?"

Turn and walk away.

Scholars agree that a complex array of social and environmental factors contributed to Provo's demise. But the consensus is that Brigham Young University delivered the death blow.

BYU's infamous "NO SEX Contract," initially instituted to keep horny undergrads upright, and enforced by a network of student spies, was an unqualified success. But when it was foisted onto the larger community an unforeseen decline in population ensued.

Now when you drive I-15 past what was once Provo, only Utah Lake remains unchanged, an enormous bowl of brown Jello.

"Looking Northwest from South Pimple Street,": • The world famous Beehive Hotel, home of the state's most pampered vegetables. • Beehive Beauty College, founded by Gordy Utah. Here, his pioneer coiffure techniques are kept alive in a "quasi-living museum." • The Beehive House, once home of pioneer hairdresser Gordy Utah. It is said that he invented the beehive hairdo within these walls. • The new, lofty Mormon Headquarters, where the Pioneer Accordion Quintet gives recitals weekly. • Beagle Gate, is yet another memorial to the "Hound of the Lord."

The Mormons

Industrious, Honest, Forthright, Peculiar

I N much the same spirit that the makers of Tang assume when informing us that their product is "the breakfast drink of the astronauts," the Mormons will tell you they are a "peculiar people." There is always a note of pride in the statement, and by their own lights, this pride is well justified.

Mormons believe that they are the sole practitioners of original Christianity, and that both spiritual authority and divine revelation, having been lost, were restored to them through the prophet Joseph Smith.

Measured against the values of society at large, this sort of makes Mormonism the triple-burger of organized religion. Only the Mormons and Jehovah's Witnesses claim publicly that they have cornered the market on truth. And around here, Mormons have all the clout. To Mormons, the Pope is a piker hedging his bets.

Even so, whether or not you accept their proprietary claims, it can't be denied that Mormons have created a culture more decent and hard-working than most.

So, if decency is your cup of Postum, join with us in offering a temperate toast: "Health, happiness, funny underwear!"

The Mormons

Industrious, Honest, Forthright, Peculiar

BOYD Bigler's lovely wife, Bambi Budge Bigler, traces her Mormon lineage back to her great-great-grandfather Boyce Enoch Budge who, along with his first wife Betty, pushed a grocery cart from Nauvoo across the plains and eventually settled and farmed the area between Bandelo and the desolate Mr. Mesa country.

Once established, at the behest of Brigham Young, Boyce Enoch and Betty obediently embarked on an unparalleled twenty-year foray of begatting that left in its wake twenty-four children and an interesting comment from Betty at the birth of number twenty-four.

"Guh, guh," she is reported to have said.

In his own time Guhguh Cecil Budge begat Bryce B. Budge, who in turn begat La Bob Budge. La Bob and his wife Bobette begat and raised seven lovely daughters of which Bambi was the second.

And even now Bambi will proudly tell you that she is of the "Budges of Bandelo."

Present-day Mormon culture has strong roots. The pioneer heritage is a tangible element in everyday life. Ancestors are revered, their traditions upheld; and the begatting goes on and on.

If Mormons have an uncommonly strong regard for their connections with the past, their reverence towards the lines of authority in the present-day organization is no less robust.

Gateway editors asked Bambi, "How do you know that your church is the only true church?"

"Well, for one thing, the Bishop told me," she replied.

"Yes Bambi, but how does he know?"

"The Stake President mentioned it to him just the other day. And not for the first time either."

Thinking that we had her, we pushed on. "Okay Bambi, but how does he know?"

"One of the Apostles told him. He has it in writing." Bambi folded her arms and smiled serenely.

Sure of our ultimate success, we pressed the question. "But where is this Apostle getting his information?"

"From the President of the Church, of course." Bambi mustered her patience.

Inwardly we rubbed our hands together. "We're sure that he's a wise man, Bambi, but who told him?"

"God," she replied.

Committed to the ideals of gracious womanhood, Bambi didn't even try for the extra point. We were grateful and have since quit arguing religion with Mormons.

An unusual result of this singular notion of absolute rightness among Mormons has been the emergence of a peculiar cultural schizophrenia. It has produced an enviable spiritual contentment, but has also created a defensiveness that verges on paranoia.

The streets of Salt Lake City and Provo are littered with professional Mormon historians, each with a bloody nose. In general, the ongoing encounter with secular society, that has been increasing along with the phenomenal growth of the church, has been a stormy one.

While they were picking up a six pack, two *Gateway* editors happened on Boyd Bigler in the parking lot of a local Safeway supermarket. Boyd was carrying a three foot club and skulking between parked cars. We approached him.

"Boyd, we just talked to your lovely wife, Bambi. What are you up to?"

"I'm protecting my family from the evils of organic evolution, the ERA, abortion, humanism, rationalism, birth control, non-Mormon archeologists and their brothers, the pornographers."

"Good job, Boyd," we called as we waved.

On the way out of the lot we noticed a well-known biologist trying to disguise himself as a dumpster. He crouched and tip-toed toward our car.

"Hey fellows. How about a lift?"

"Where are you headed?"

"The North Pole ... Nevada ... out of here!"

Like the practice of baptism for the dead, the world-wide missionary program arises from the Mormons' belief that they are in possession of the absolute truth as revealed by God. The missionary program doesn't merely comprise an attempt to expand Mormon influence, but is also a generous offer to share the goodies.

The proselytizing effort has more than doubled in the last several years with predictably dramatic results in the market-place.

When the church announced increases in the number of missionaries being deployed, stock in companies manufacturing white socks and off-the-rack suits with pre-shined bottoms rose accordingly. Needless to say, the smart money made a killing.

The fact that this pervasive attitude of certainty and rightness is held by a majority of people in the state has some curious effects on the non-Mormon population. Random and severe itching of the palms, thighs and neck (Brick wall syndrome) is a commonplace response to the situation. Crossed eyes combined with snuffling in the nostrils (Gentile's whimper) has recently reached epidemic proportions.

Hovering over the Latter-day Saint's horizon is the revealed word of God on the topic of moderation. Apparently, He's for it.

"The Word of Wisdom" is the name given to this portion of Mormon scripture. Among other things, it advises moderation in the consumption of meat, and orders complete abstinence from hot drinks, tobacco and alcohol. It doesn't mention amphetamines or sex.

Nobody took it very seriously in the early days, but as the church moved from its vital youthful days to the present it became progressively important.

Today, this clean living face that it chooses to present to the world has also become the standard by which individuals are judged. A person is better off robbing a gas station than smoking in public. A person's moral rectitude index plummets at the mention of "strong drink" as it's known, or tobacco.

Spotting the wayward Mormon requires a keen eye.

"What'll it be, Mac?"

"Strong drink … uhh … with rocks."
"Check."

But most Mormons don't often stray. The flock is remarkably intact. As Boyd Bigler put it, "There's nowhere to go but down."

Green Punch

Divine intervention was the source of the mandatory beverage of Mormon weddings. The formula for green punch was revealed to Brigham Young on a Wednesday.

Do you know the
Ten Warning Signals of the
Missionary?

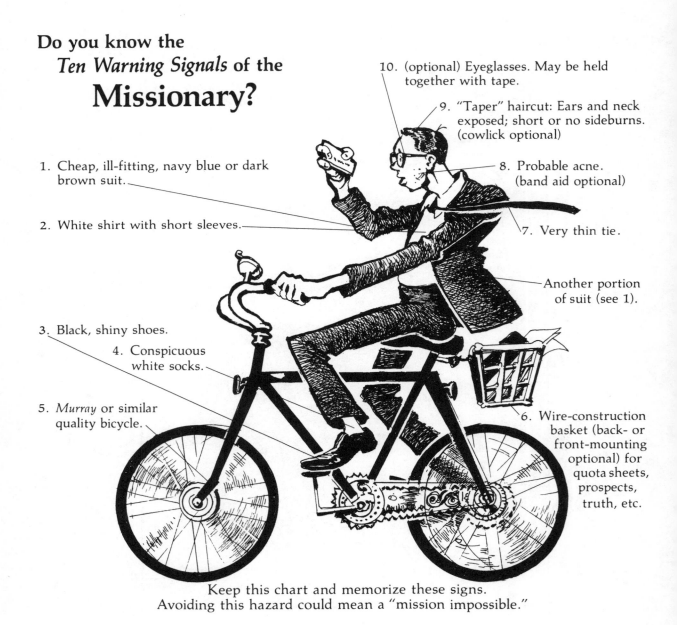

10. (optional) Eyeglasses. May be held together with tape.

9. "Taper" haircut: Ears and neck exposed; short or no sideburns. (cowlick optional)

1. Cheap, ill-fitting, navy blue or dark brown suit.

8. Probable acne. (band aid optional)

2. White shirt with short sleeves.

7. Very thin tie.

Another portion of suit (see 1).

3. Black, shiny shoes.

4. Conspicuous white socks.

5. *Murray* or similar quality bicycle.

6. Wire-construction basket (back- or front-mounting optional) for quota sheets, prospects, truth, etc.

Keep this chart and memorize these signs.
Avoiding this hazard could mean a "mission impossible."

He Used to Play at the Cinegrill

Food sculptor Cyprus Daln's interpretation of the angel caps the Salt Lake Temple, and refers to the prophecy that Moroni will play "Lady of Spain" to announce the millenium. The beautiful gold foil wrapping belies the rich milk chocolate from which this distinctive landmark is molded.

Mormon Outcasts

Certain elements within the Mormon Church have created controversy and conflict by asserting that it is impossible to be both a good Mormon and a drug-crazed, commie, homo pimp.

Predictably, drug-crazed, commie, homo pimps within the church have withdrawn, injured and angry, claiming that they are every bit as good as their neighbors. Even so, as a group, their attendance at young adults' functions has dropped off sharply.

Although the chasm of misunderstanding is a difficult one to bridge, the common ground between them offers hope for reconciliation:

Both groups are firm in their belief that it is impossible to be a good Mormon and a Democrat.

The Word of Wisdom

This decade heralds the century and a half mark since Joseph Smith received notice from above concerning (and denouncing) excess, and a nice round fifty years since the repeal of prohibition. *Gateway* editors were on hand to record the celebration hosted by the League of Jack Mormons (L'JAM) in honor of these controversial events.

The Mormon Tabernacle Accordion

The world famous Mormon Tabernacle Choir says "cheese" in front of the equally famous tabernacle accordion. Hauled across the plains piece-by-piece, this remarkable instrument is held together entirely with band-aids. Public recitals are held daily during "Peppy Hour" (4-6 p.m.). Summer's annual "polka fest" draws dozens of enthusiasts.

Cathedrals and Wardhouses —Architectural Comparisons

Lofty achievements pock the history of religious architecture.

In a spirit of snide mockery, *Gateway* editors have assembled a brief comparative collection. Photographs depicting some of the treasures of the capitals of Europe and Utah have been callously overlooked in favor of contrast. Turn your attention to the virtues of the brick.

The Family

The basic unit of our unique culture is that bastion of goodliness, the nuclear family. Although a close look at statistics on divorce, child abuse, teen pregnancy, yellow wax buildup and fratricide might test one's faith a teeny bit, it's common knowledge that everything's just super.

A Message from Above

The Book of Mormon chronicles the history of pre-columbian America and clears up the question of the origin of the American Indian, or "Lamanites" as it calls them. Among other things, it explains that the red pigmentation of the Indians' complexion is the result of God's wrath—a curse, as it were.

Fortunately, the Indians seem to take it all in stride. "Palefaces have empty teepees between ears," quipped Brent Fox to a *Gateway* investigator.

Below, Brent pays a spontaneous mid-morning visit on Bishop Bigler. Brunch is beef jerky and Fresca.

Myths of Mormonism Dispelled

Many commonly held beliefs about Mormonism result in barriers of confusion between the faithful and newcomers to the area. With the intention of dismantling these obstructions, *Gateway* editors interviewed the well-known authority on everything Mormon, Bishop Boyd Bigler. The session took place in the congenial atmosphere of Bishop Bigler's rumpus room.

Gateway editors chose the question/answer format because, as Dr. Joyce Brothers has demonstrated time and again, it automatically reduces even the most meaningful information to garbage.

Q. Isn't it true that all Mormons are oddball, weirdo freaks who have horns growing out of their heads; that they keep at least a dozen wives each, send their babies to Cuba for training in techniques of world conquest, participate in lurid sex orgies in their so-called "temples," never smoke, drink neither coffee nor alcohol, and wear strange underwear called garments?

A. Well ... yes and no.

Q. And isn't it also true that Joseph Smith was in fact a member of the international communist conspiracy, that he left a string of unpaid traffic tickets between New York and Illinois, and slept with a stuffed brontosaurus that he referred to as "Noodles"?

A. Uh ... I don't have any information on the traffic tickets, but I'm sure that if he got one now and then he would have ....

Q. And isn't it also documented that on May 4th, 1833 he made contact with aliens bent on altering the brains and kidneys of the entire human race?

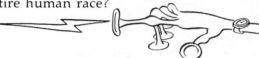

A. ... Maybe a ticket for double parking here and there. I really don't ....

Q. And furthermore, is it not the case that at this very moment Church authorities are secretly plotting to deprive Americans of their most cherished rights and freedoms?

A. Hardly. I'm sure they're eating lunch this time of day.

Q. Finally, can you deny the truth of these affidavits proving that Mormon fashion designer, Mona Rae Dawn LaFevre, in collusion with Joseph Stalin, foisted the puff sleeve pioneer dress on the public as a way of weakening the strength and spirit of the American people; and that furthermore, as a child, she ate Dog Yummies on at least two occasions?

A. As far as I know Mona Rae's diet is ...

Q. Then you don't know for sure?

A. Well ....

Tribute to Mormon Women

We pause at this point to pay our respects to a beleaguered but courageous group: *Mormon women.*

They pulled handcarts across the plains and over the Rockies. They worked alongside the men in the fields while successfully managing households and giving birth to endless litters of little Saints.

They didn't complain.

And they're still at it, a classic case of a group that shoulders enormous responsibility without a requisite amount of authority. It appears to the outsider like a terribly unstable situation. We plug our ears and think, "This could blow at any second"; but still they don't complain. We have no alternative but to stand back and admire these persevering ladies.

When you're married to a patriarch it doesn't matter how fast you run—you always place second.

But maybe in the end, that will turn out to be a winner.

This Utah family finds togetherness in the simple homely pleasures during their big night out on the town; proving once again that the best things in life are free.

The Lifestyle

And the Word Was "Nice"

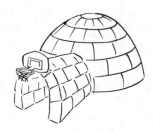

BOYD Bigler and his lovely wife, Bambi Budge Bigler, greeted us warmly at the entrance to their ranch style suburban home. As we were escorted into the living room we admired the Eskimo-Mediterranean decor and met their six charming children, Boyd Jr., LaVoy, El Heber, Candy, Mindy and Rulon, all under the age of four and a half years. We took a seat on a block of ice.

Well Boyd, how would you describe your lifestyle?"

"It's nice. No question about it."

We turned to Mrs. Bigler, "What do you think, Bambi?"

Well, I'd say it's very, very, very nice."

El Heber said "Wah."

We agreed and spent a nice half hour chatting with the Biglers.

Consider: Our arts and entertainments are nice. We have nice families who eat nice food and have nice children. We are known for our nice wide streets with nice curbing and nice gutters. Nice pizza parlors and nice carports abound.

Contrast this with say, California, where the key word is "fun"; where you find fun couples and fun curbs and gutters and so on.

A fun lifestyle is O.K., but in our opinion, "nice" has "fun" beat by a mile, maybe more.

The Lifestyle

Fun, Family, Food, Fine Arts, Obedience

FROM the geranium pots of Temple Square to the flesh-pots of Sandy, the lifestyle enjoyed by Utahns is unique ... peculiar ... wonderful.

It would be difficult to overstate the Mormon Church's influence on the Utah lifestyles of both members and gentiles. Since it's a nice church, a nice lifestyle seems to be the natural result.

It's almost as if Moroni, atop the Salt Lake Temple, is playing his accordion to the tune of ... say, "You Light Up My Life," and that this melody reaches into every nook, each cranny in the state, setting the tone and providing the ground from which our lifestyle emerges. We think that you'll agree that "You Light Up My Life" is a very nice tune.

If there is a problem, it is simply that in order to turn it off, you have to drive all the way to Nevada. Mozart lovers tend to end up in institutions. But it's a small price to pay, and the institutions, of course, are very nice.

"Lifestyle" seems to come into sharper focus on those occasions when people turn their thoughts to a night on the town. So *Gateway* editors arranged to observe Boyd and Bambi Bigler on the celebration of their fifth wedding anniversary.

A secluded and well-lit booth at a fine ice cream emporium was the setting for the first stop of an evening of pleasure in Utah's capital city.

"Fifteen plastic roses! Oh Boyd, I bet they last for time and all eternity!"

"Wind and water erosion will eventually do them in, Snookie."

"You're sweet ... and thank you."

Warming to his subject, Boyd continued, "Even the most durable substances, when exposed to the elements for periods of ..."

A plump and pert adolescent dressed in a combo pioneer woman-upstairs maid-train conductor outfit with a little sign on her chest proclaiming, "Hi! I'm Brenda," bounced to the booth. "Pig's repast for two. Extra nuts."

"Looks delish, Brenda. Thank you."

The Biglers raised their tiny spoons.

Stop number two was the Seagull State Quilting Bee Championship Playoff. The

44

arena was packed with frenzied fans, and Boyd, in an expansive moment had purchased tickets right on center court.

The Biglers fought their way through the stadium as the teams warmed up. The ladies jogged in place, chose thimbles and patted each other on the rear, exuding a feeling of control and confidence.

Wearing pink fuzzy slippers, the Bandelo Wolverines had dominated the quilting competitions for the past three years. They were formidable—a polyester-covered mountain of granite.

Confronting them with a characteristic-ally cocky giant-killer attitude were those ladies in apricot fuzzy slippers, the notorious Bulldogs out of Dryheave.

Both teams were smart and tough. The aggressively tiered beehive hairdos glistened under the stadium lights. The rules were simple: Crush the opponent.

The whistle sounded and needles flashed. Pom-pom toting cheerleaders fanned the flames.

"BEE-O-BEE-DEE-UNT
BEE-O-BEE-DEE-UNT
STITCH-THAT-BULL-DOG
TO-HER-SO-FA
BEE-O-BEE-DEE-UNT"

In the third quarter the Wolverines came unstitched, making way for the new champs.

The Biglers decided against taking the midnight tour of the Osmond Studios as they had planned. Instead they drove home, presumably to work a little on replenishing the earth.

"It was a nice evening, wasn't it, Bambi?"
"It was very nice, Boyd."

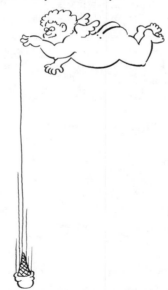

"Boyd...what's the meaning of life?"
"I'll tell you later, Bambi."
"Okee dokee."

Slogans, Mottos and Symbols

Utahns have a lot of spirit. You ask yourself, "What does that mean?" It's a reasonable question because nobody knows for sure.

Even if it can't be defined, it might be possible to describe it, and in a foolish moment *Gateway* editors decided to try.

The essence of the type of spirit that we are attempting to get at is contained in the pom-pom, the energetic "Hooray," the leaping cheerleader; in short, enthusiastic and thoughtless allegiances to teams, schools, churches, institutions, geographical areas or just about anything.

Where you have spirit you also find slogans, mottos and an assortment of symbols that serve as a rallying point for the faithful. Here's a quick look at Utah's interesting collection.

Hiss, Boom, Bah Humbug.

State slogan: "Largest Women"

This slogan is a response to Idaho's "Famous Potatoes" license plates. That "can do" spirit nudged Utahns into a friendly competition with our neighbors to the north. A statewide contest resulted in thousands of slogan ideas.

Cloy and FayDawn Budge were selected to judge the entries because of their wide experience in R.V. maintenance and grocery checking, respectively. We have included the top three entries with commentary by the Budges.
1. "Largest Women"
As Cloy put it, "We're proud of our girls and don't care who knows it."
2. "Best in the West"
"This one combined cheerful mindlessness with an admirable amount of spunk," remarked Cloy. FayDawn added, "It has a 'my dad can beat up your dad' feel to it that almost put it ahead of the number one choice."
3. "Nice Place"
"Number three really captured our hearts," said FayDawn. But in the end it was judged to be a bit too poetic.

State bird: Beagle

Utah has the distinction of being the only state to have a dog as the state bird. (See Legend and Lore section.) We know, we know, it's damn peculiar. But we are peculiar people.

State fight song: "Utah, None Dare Call It Idaho"

It's set to the tune of "Ebb Tide" and sung with great fervor at the semi-annual statewide pep rallies. A spontaneous invasion of Arizona had to be quelled on one occasion after an especially rousing rendition.

State motto: "How High?"

When Uncle Sam says "Jump!" what Utahn wouldn't say, "How High?"

State flower: Seagull

Utah has the distinction of being the only state to have a bird as the state flower.

State seal:

The seal of the great state of Utah recalls our proud heritage. An encircled beehive rampant on a field of blue honors frontier hairdresser, Gordy Utah. The state motto, "How High?" adds meaning to this powerful symbol.

State dog: Sego Lily

Utah has the distinction of being the only state to have a flower as the state dog.

West Valley Cultural Center —"...And There Shall Be Culture"

Utah boasts dozens of local cultural centers where citizens flock to relax, socialize, and share with one another the rich heritage of the Beehive State. In the $3.6-million dollar example shown below, the roaming pioneer mindscape has been united with the unique Utah landscape in a perfect blend of art, architecture, and simple home-grown values. The soaring lines of this edifice, nestled in a park-like setting, create a vision of motion in immobility. Once inside, a fantasy land of recreational as well as contemplative activities are available, including an art alcove, a poetry niche, and a gunnery range. The hidden parking-lot underneath doubles as a drive-in theatre and R.V. park. The second floor features video arcades, snowmobiling and dirt-bike expositions, as well as the inspiring "Hall of Freedoms." This imposing structure is topped off with the world's only 200 lane bowling alley/ice cream palace. In front of the center is a monumental fountain; dubbed "The Pin" by admirers, it was donated by fountain-enthusiast, local tanner and philanthropist, O.C. Brunswick.

The Big Delivery (The Count is 3 and 2...and...)

The scores are in, the tallies have been tabulated. Now the entire state casts a proud if somewhat envious glance at Utah County. They've scored big with a higher birth rate than any other underdeveloped country in the world.

Asked to express his feelings, Boyd Bigler remarked, "I could just bust my buttons."

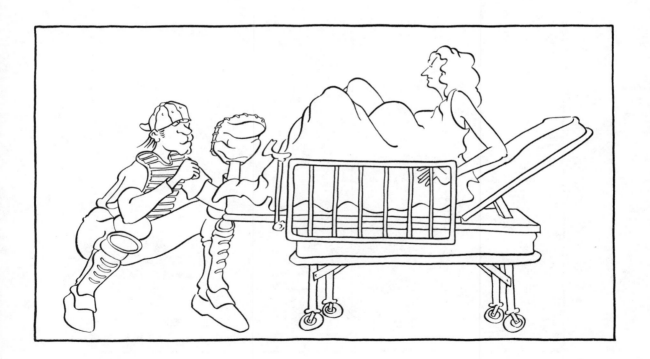

Life's Important Lessons

The strength of the Utah family is legendary. Life's important lessons are learned therein.

The Grim Reaper

Where you find life (like say, in Utah, for instance) you're also going to encounter death. It's not nice.

The absence of niceness has led to a widespread disbelief in the reality of death. But sooner or later the Grim Reaper knocks.

Another loved one turns belly-up and claims the status of dearly departed.

There is need for times of remembrance. Virtues are recalled and savored.

Sometimes vices are recalled and savored too.

Where to Go—Lube Jobs

Utah is blessed with a virtual plethora of lube job offerings. Along the Wasatch Front a number of centers are justified in recommending themselves as first rate:

The Lube Job Conspiracy and *Keepsake Lube Jobs*, both in the downtown area, transcend the ordinary with their sensitive lube treatments. For the especially discerning, *Lubes Capri* can field your oil needs. And when you're looking for something a little different, *Fiesta Lube* will grease your sensibilities with just a touch of "Old Meh-Hee-Ko."

The cutting edge of current lube job trends are intelligently explored at either *Image Lube* or *The Lube Job Connection*. And tradition-minded *McKay O'Donnell Lube Jobs* slides home with an extended history of conservative lube job excellence.

Finally, for that late evening after the symphony lube job, it's *Scampi's*, of course.

Utah Drivers

A lot has been said about the Utah driver.
Perhaps the less said, the better.

Utah Industries Map

Many visitors to Utah are stunned by the rapidly expanding industrial/technological growth and breakthroughs. Local leaders proudly proclaim that soon no one in the state will remain unaffected by the rapid changes. As Boyd Bigler says: "At this rate, you'll hardly recognize the place in twenty years."

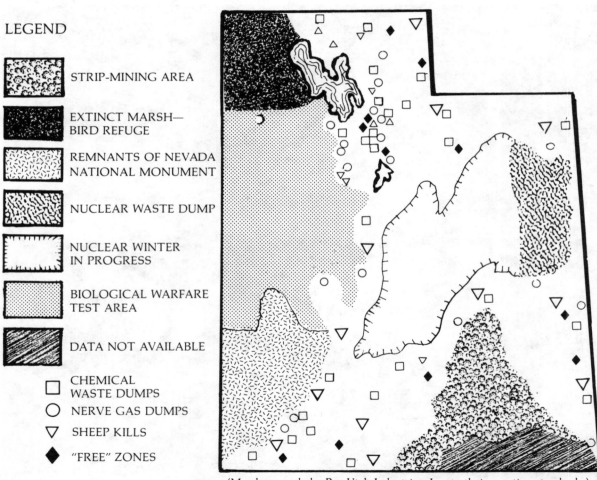

LEGEND

STRIP-MINING AREA

EXTINCT MARSH—
BIRD REFUGE

REMNANTS OF NEVADA
NATIONAL MONUMENT

NUCLEAR WASTE DUMP

NUCLEAR WINTER
IN PROGRESS

BIOLOGICAL WARFARE
TEST AREA

DATA NOT AVAILABLE

☐ CHEMICAL
WASTE DUMPS

○ NERVE GAS DUMPS

▽ SHEEP KILLS

◆ "FREE" ZONES

(Map base made by Pro-Utah Industries, Inc. to their exacting standards.)

Utah's Exploding Industrial Scene—Nukebonzo Corporation

A well known financial journal describes Nukebonzo Corporation as an attractive high-risk venture with explosive potential: "Nukebonzo has successfully welded ideas from the 'holistic movement' to a nuts and bolts practical program of nuclear genocide."

The Talk Show

The Salt Lake area has experienced a proliferation of radio talk-shows in recent years that has culminated in the enormously successful, "Save My Bacon, Dr. Crawlspace." The hostess, "Dr." Irma Crawlspace provides a genuine service by proffering a spectrum of nuggets from the accumulated wisdom of the social sciences.

A section from the famous Gary Gilmore tape is presented below.

Humanism

A Warning for Travelers

The political "New Right" has a strong foothold in Utah. A symptom of this style of thought is their desire to impose fundamentalist standards on people who don't share them.

For example, anti-humanism has become a hallmark of the "New Right." There is much confusion, however, as to what humanism is. Webster defines "humanist" as "a person who adheres to a modern non-theistic rationalist movement that holds that man is capable of self-fulfillment and ethical conduct without recourse to super-naturalism." On the other hand, large numbers of Utahns define "humanist" as "pornographer" or "baby killer."

So if you're driving through, don't chat about cable TV. The locals might get testy.

57

Science—Ice Cream Research

Top level research conducted in congenial surroundings characterizes the Utah scientific community.

Gateway editors contacted Linus El Rod Foote of Brigham Young University's Division of Bio-recreation. We queried Dr. Foote about research in progress.

"Presently we are engaged in testing ice cream on rats," he told us. "Much of this is theory, but preliminary results indicate that they favor strawberry over caramel pecan."

"Hmmmmm," we said.

"The technical difficulties involved in getting the pecans through the syringes have been staggering."

Fascinated, we pressed on.

"The future?" Dr. Foote's eyes glazed slightly as he looked beyond us. "The digital nose spray project promises renewed hope for world-wide nasal relief. At this point however, finding rats with large enough nostrils has been a major road block. In fact, the ballroom dancer cloning project has been temporarily abandoned in favor of a crash program in rat nostril augmentation."

"That is serious," we agreed. "One final question then, Doctor. As a biologist at BYU, what do you think about evolution?"

His gaze was steady as he replied, "Personally, I prefer the caramel pecan."

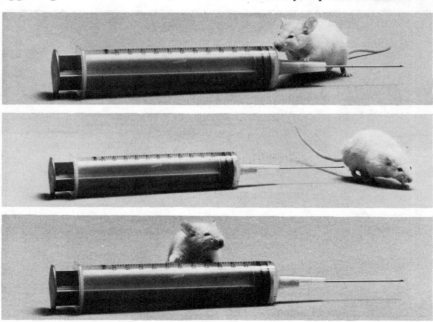

Ice Cream Abusers

Once the scourge of ghetto parlors, ice cream abuse no longer confines its ugly tentacles to others, ... say, jazz musicians.

It could happen in your neighborhood. It could happen in your family. It could happen to you ... and probably will.

Maybe you know someone, an uncle, a sister, a service rep who is struggling with this vice. Well, tough for them I guess.

When you're hooked on ice cream you're in for the hassle of your life.

Sports

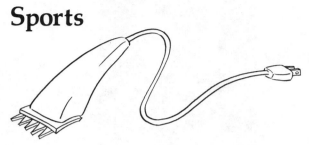

Men need to know about sports. In fact, to be among the top finishers in Utah's social superbowl requires a dedication to both spectator and participation sports. If you're not a hoopster or hurler, a gridder, a slugger, a slatster or nimrod, a netster or linkster, you might as well throw in the towel, because you'll be trounced in the preseason and relegated to the dubious niche of bench jockey in Utah's sports-oriented culture.

Strangely, the institution that shoulders the responsibility for this ordering of society is the neighborhood barber shop.

In order to observe the odd rituals that perpetuate this curious phenomenon, *Gateway* editors accompanied Boyd Bigler on a recent visit to his barbershop. Boyd confided that he knows almost nothing about sports and has been faking it for years. LaDave, a barber and more importantly, guardian of class distinctions has, Boyd tells us, become increasingly suspicious of Boyd's devotion to sports in recent months.

Several hurdles have to be successfully cleared in this social tilt. If the patron chokes, he will leave the shop looking like Rookie of the Year, a marked man, ostracized and shamed.

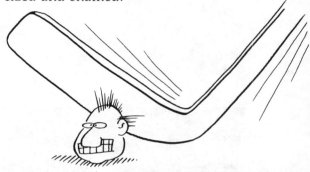

As we parked the Buick Le Sabre in front of LaDave's shop, Boyd expressed his apprehension.

"I'm in a slump today. What if I strike out?"

We offered a reassuring smile.

Hurdle # 1: Magazine Selection

Boyd entered seated himself and uttered a throaty grunt of satisfaction. He assumed an expression of nebulous good will and greeted LaDave.

"Howzitt hangin', LaDave?"

LaDave managed a noncommital nod and returned his attention to the patron in the chair and the ongoing discussion of the high points surrounding the 1938 Joe Louis-Max Schmeling bout.

Boyd turned to the magazine rack. Confronting him were copies of *People*, *National Geographic* and *Field and Stream*. He wavered, indecisive, then gathered his wits and calmly plucked the *Field and Stream* from its altar. We quit holding our breath.

Hurdle #2: Establishing Oneself as a Knowledgeable Spectator

"Hey," Boyd interjected, "did you see the Packers-Colts game last Thursday? What a squeaker."

LaDave snorted. Adopting a didactic tone, he said, "That was Friday, Boyd, and 71 to 7 isn't a squeaker."

Well, I was glued to *my* chair," said Boyd.

In Boyd's defense, we should point out that he was referring to real teams that both play the same sport, and to a game that actually occurred. It might have been worse.

"What have you been doing, Boyd?"

"Hanging around the Pro Shop, mainly."

"Hm..." said LaDave.

"Just yesterday I bought a dozen pucks."

"Hmmm..." said LaDave.

"Nice to have a few extras on board in case one gets lost in the outfield, huh?" Boyd's eyes were beginning to show an edge of panic.

"Hmmmm..." said LaDave.

"I got the extra large this year. Best puck you can buy. Hand sewn," he said pleadingly.

LaDave kicked the clippers up to high. In four seconds Boyd had a jagged mohawk with adroit tufting on the left side. "You're finished, Bigler. Get out."

We dragged Boyd screaming from LaDave's. Halfway out the door he turned back. "Wanna hear a great lesbian joke I heard the other day?"

"Too little, too late, Boyd," said LaDave. "Next."

Hurdle #3: The Firing Line

Boyd climbed into the chair. "Crew cut with white-walls." LaDave nodded approval and revved up his clippers.

Seagull Forking Tips

(Never let the seagull know you're afraid of him.)

1 — The Approach

2 — Stance and Backswing

3 — Delivery

4 — Follow-through

Hunting Season...Duck!

More than any other outdoor event, open season on domestic ducks makes the Utah sportsman's blood run hot with primal urges. Whether it's a shotgun at ten paces or the more challenging bow shoot, fine sport is enjoyed by all.

The Wily Coyote

The desert country of southern Utah manages to support a variety of thirsty life. Among the larger mammals that survive mom nature's questionable hospitality is a smallish wild dog that looks like a toy wolf. It's called the coyote. Coyotes often visit campsites in search of food.

The coyote is a central character in many legends of local Indian tribes. Ranchers and sheepmen have endless stories about the cunning and intelligence of this remarkable animal.

We're not going to tell you any of them.

Ski Utah

Utah is world-famous for its snow—said to be the lightest powder in the world.

Conveniently located between Colorado and Nevada, Utah's pristine slopes are a handy thirty-seven hours by car from Kennedy International Airport.

The Face Plant

The Face Plant is one of the more difficult hot-dogging techniques to master. Usually, after two or three successful attempts, the skier has a hard time remembering which way is up, let alone how to put on his skis. After a season or two of Face Planting, afficionados often turn to state politics.

Athletics at Brigham Young University

Athletics at BYU are pretty much the same as everything else at BYU.

Cuisine

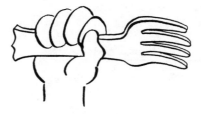

The gastro scene in Utah is a product of a rich heritage that is woven through the historical fabric of the state. In fact, Utahns have been eating since the very early days, some say since before statehood.

More recently, studies indicate that Utah has a higher number of hearty eaters per capita than any state in the Union except Alabama, and ranks a very respectable fifth in the category of serious eating.

After all, wasn't it a Utahn, Boyd Bigler, who first asked, "Why did the broasted chicken cross the road?"

The Pork Cook-off

No annual foodstuffs competition stops more hearts than the keenly competitive *Utah Pork Cook-off*.

Every county fields several teams of crack homemakers hoping to garner top honors.

Training begins in early spring and culminates in a crescendo of pork cookery at the mid-summer contest. Emotions run high.

The victorious team gains more than just prestige. They also get a loving cup.

DISCIPLINING THE PIG

DICING THE ONIONS

WAITING FOR THE MICROWAVE

MEETING THE JUDGES

RELAXING BEFORE THE RETURNS

ACCEPTING THE AWARD

Eating Out

Fat Bob's, Utah's hugely successful home-owned fast food franchise, delivers more burgers to the hungry tummies of the area's population than any other similar enterprise. Their domination of the local market is due to a specialty item, the Reverence Burger, which features an all beef pattie pressed into the shape of the Mormon Tabernacle Choir.

As part of our investigation, *Gateway* editors purchased one of Fat Bob's burgers, popped it into a zip-lock baggie and sent it off to Tech Du Labs for analysis. The results? A Fat Bob Burger has the nutritional value of 3.6 jelly beans. (Analysis does not include the poly foam container.) We were pleasantly surprised.

The Gourmet's Corner—Goes Great with Miniature Marshmallows

Utahns are famous for having created a local cuisine from the state's varied culinary opportunities. Donna Lou Morgan, Utah's premier gourmet and cuisine critic offers up a new and breathtaking *hors d'oeuvre* recipe.

"I just grab an empty Skippy jar and head for the Jordan River," explains Mrs. Morgan. And a word or two of caution: "Don't forget to poke holes in the lid."

Those with a penchant for gracious living will want to tease the palates of their guests with a rasher of "Bugs Rio Jordan."

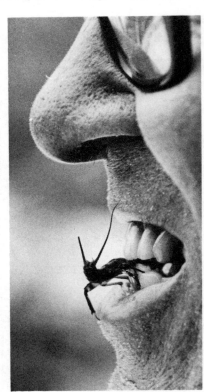

Bugs Rio Jordan

Bugs, 2 cups.
Cook until dead.

Serve chilled with popcorn,
miniature marshmallows,
or nose-clips.

Bon Appetit!

The Arts

"Look, Bambi." Boyd Bigler pointed a quivering finger at the larger than lifesize bust of Utah poet, Voyda Richards Cannon Smith Young.

Recently acquired by the Utah Fine Museum of Arts as a significant addition to its perishables collection, the seven foot countenance dominated the gallery.

Delicately hewn from a twelve-hundred pound slab of spam by Utahn, Avard Alvin, the sculpture transcends likeness to give us a glimpse into the soul of the poet.

"The craftsmanship is superb," remarked Boyd. "Notice the sensitive handling of the liver spots, the finely chiseled mole."

"I'd never noticed it before," said Bambi, "but Voyda looks a little like Abraham Lincoln."

The arts in Utah are vital, growing, sometimes they even emit gases.

The Symphony Geld

Salt Lake City, sometimes considered a center for both the performing and visual arts, has witnessed the introduction of a new wrinkle into its cultural scene. A regulation is currently in force that requires symphony players and conductors to be "fixed."

Symphony Guild Veep, Boyd Bigler, claims that reports of grumbling within symphony circles are false. "There seems to be an attitude of acceptance," Boyd told us. "In fact, they are strangely docile about the whole thing."

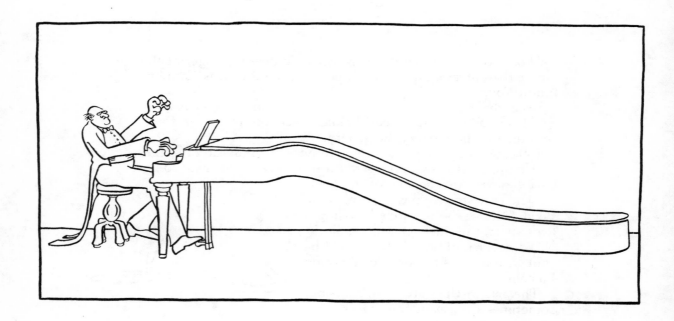

Grass Roots

Yes, we have Repertory Dance Theatre, Ballet West, and the Utah Symphony, and all three enjoy national reputations.

Sounds remarkable? But wait, there's more. The real strength of Utah's fine arts lies in its amateur organizations and grass roots efforts.

Utah's Poet Laureate — Darkling Dowager

No book that pretends to display Utah's variety would be complete without mention of our grand old lady of high culture, San Juan County's dowager word-smith, Voyda Richards Cannon Smith Young. Poet Young, author of the acclaimed volumes, *Lizards and Lollipops; In Yet Such Times as These, Still too, Another Mountain; Rival Gangs of Zion Sing La Lu* and *Darkling Gabfest*, graciously consented to an interview.

Gateway editors engaged Boyd Bigler, a recognized authority on the modern verse of southeastern Utah to conduct the session. The intriguing results follow.

B.B.: 'Lo, Voyda.
Voyda: 'Lo, Boyd.
B.B.: How's Pa Cannon?
Voyda: Gout's worse.
B.B.: Darn shame.
Voyda: Yup.
B.B.: Tell me Voyda, do you agree that formal elements in your verse combine with a subliminal lyricism to enhance tonal themes through a subtle cacophony of alliterative schemes that are interwoven with carefully controlled metric shifts, but occasionally at the expense of internal textural idioms?
Voyda: I expect so, Boyd.
B.B.: Say 'lo to Pa Cannon.
Voyda: Will do.

A selection of some of Voyda's best loved verse follows.

The Darkling Tater Dog

My eyes are peeled lemons.
My guts are spliced baloney.
My bum is made from bowling balls.
I think I am a phoney.

The Darkling Lungfish

Twilight, like cornflakes
Crackles around me
As I sit
Honked off in my chair
And tweeze a hair from a mole,
(My knees sort of pink).
Bushed, I smile wanly
And watch my lungfish
As he cavorts
Uncaring in his bowl.
Sometimes I wish
He weren't so gung-ho.

The Darkling Sincerity of Daddy's Farm

None can compare
With the sincerity
Of Daddy's farm.
The barn stands red like a barn.
With broadsides.
The silo juts toward heaven
Like a silo.
And chickens dot the barnyard
Like chickens
Dotting the barnyard.
The mighty horse
Thunders about,
His neck straining
Like the neck of a horse.

Indeed, the cow
Grazes the pasture
With the contentment of a cow.
Who would feign to know
Her glassy-eyed secrets?
Or thunder about, neck straining?
They remind me more
Of simple field mice
Like the simple field mice
On Daddy's farm.
We've got a million of 'em.

Darkling Shoe

I saw a tennis shoe lying in the road,
I saw a tennis shoe lying in the road,
I saw a tennis shoe lying in the road,
It was nearly one point five meters from the curb.

Darkling Winter

Alas!
The winter comes
And
This poet weeps
Capital
Letters.

The Darkling Cow

Of all the folks
    I ever knew
The very best
    could only moo.

"Brigham's Unit"—one of the natural wonders of the
Hot Rocks area of Utah.

The Land

Mountains, Deserts, Forests, Waste Dumps

YOU are probably expecting the mandatory paragraph about roots; about how the people are the land and vice-versa.

A square-jawed blurb on sacrifice generally follows the part about roots. The high cost of winning the land is recounted in heroic prose. (Mine eyes have seen many development packages.) Melodic strains from the National Anthem begin to waft through the mushy regions of our consciousness as we search expectantly for the photograph of the wrinkled old farmer with a double handful of rich loamy soil.

We're going to stay as far away from that as possible.

Sticking with the facts then, let's just note that for the most part the land is sort of medium brown, and sometimes, in Utah, it almost seems to glow.

The Land

Mountains, Deserts, Forests, Waste Dumps

Long ago, much of Utah was covered by a vast inland sea. Lake Bonneville, as it was named by the dinosaurs, extended west into Nevada and north where it lapped at the city limits of Preston, Idaho. All that remains of this once majestic body of water is a highly saline natural sewage treatment plant. Most of Utah's residents live on land that was once the domain of the primitive creatures of the deep. The huge dry lakebed that remains is known as the Nice Basin and covers the western third of the state.

The Nice Basin is bordered on the east by the rugged Wasatch Range (as it was named by the dinosaurs). Beyond the mountains in the north of the state, the Uinta Mountains rear their lofty peaks half-way to the Celestial Kingdom.

The highest mountain in the state, Peak Experience (13,987 feet) is occupied at its summit by a sage who understands the secrets of how to select the right home computer for your personal needs, and will impart his wisdom to anyone willing to make the climb.

In the southeast, the Colorado, the Green, the San Juan and the San Rafael rivers cut mighty gorges through the radioactive Mr. Mesa country, rushing south through confluence and tailings onward to Plutonium State Park and from there to their final resting place at Lake Powell. Glen Canyon Dam, which created the lake, is a superbly engineered clot in the Colorado River Basin that draws visitors from virtually miles around.

"Wonderland" is a term that is often applied to Utah. Bambi Budge Bigler's young cousin, Bork Baker Budge maintains that this is because travelers are constantly wondering how much longer it will take to get to Nevada. Utahns however, know Bork for what he is—an agent of the devil and a smart ass.

In fact, Utah is a wonderland. It's a scenic wonderland, a winter wonderland, maybe even a summer or autumn wonderland. If you read the brochures that can be picked up at any motel, you will discover that there is hardly a type of wonderland that Utah isn't.

Now consider the total land mass of the state of Utah. Recently, and from all indications just for the heck of it, the prestigious Department of Geology at Brigham Young University (as it was named by the dinosaurs) calculated with the aid of their sophisticated computer OBEDIAC, that if you laid them end to end, using all the available land, Utah could accommodate 5,201,602,564,483 packages of Twinkies. At two to a package, that's over ten trillion Twinkies.

Further studies undertaken in the spirit of, "Why the flip not?" indicated that this number of Twinkies would contain on the close order of 627,000,000,023 pounds of creamy center.

Quick to see the benefits of what had started as pure research, key members of the Utah Legislature are currently proposing a bill to implement this great work. As Rep. Horace Nesbitt (R. No Gas) has pointed out, "It is now within our power to cover the state with Twinkies. Who among you dare stand in the way of the good work?"

But there is opposition. Detractors of the "Twinkies Project" as it has come to be known, point out that there wouldn't be any room left for ballroom dancing. Utahns await the results of the debate.

Beyond partisan concerns, Utahns love this promised land. Brigham Young told them that they had better promise that they would. If nothing else, Utah is a land of many promises.

"O Beautiful for Translucent Skies..."

A view of Sandy, Utah during a temperature inversion. A consensus of natives and visitors alike agree that this is the best time to view Sandy.

Glowing Debris…A Bright Spot on the Map!

Plutonium National Park

REDDY KILOTON SEZ:

'Howdy, Folks!'

...Welcome to

PLUTONIUM
NATIONAL PARK

More Than 9,000 Square Miles of Radiant Wonderland!
OUR JOB IS TO SERVE YOU!
YOUR JOB IS TO HAVE A NICE DAY!

...and you WILL have a nice day if you'll just observe a few simple rules.

ENTERING THE PARK: There are any number of entrances to the park, but the most popular are those at Glowing Debris (East), Nosebleed (South) and Hackenspit (West). These three towns offer food and lodging services.

Due to the BLM approved wilderness characteristics of the park, the Yellowcake Kawliga Scenic Highway, the Black Bridges County Monument and RV Dump and the U-235 R.R. are all being phased out under the Post-Atomic Wilderness Act.

SERVICES: Glowing Debris, Green Lung, Hackenspit and Nosebleed all boast a multitude of private De-Tox and Care and Burn Centers. The DOE Free-burn Clinic is at Park Headquarters, located near the old townsite of Tailings. Fuel for your vehicle is widely available. Lodging and,

surprisingly, food is also offered, whether you're merely lusting after a Glo-Cone from Goodys or a three month snooze at the Eternal Dusk Motor Inn. More substantial meals are offered at all Atomic Cafes.

WHAT TO SEE: Since there are more than 6,235 miles of pavement in the park, many thrilling vistas are accessible to the RV enthusiast who is reluctant to leave the safety of his motor home. For the history buff, a scale model of the original "nuclear waste repository" has been restored across from Park HQ. Barring unforeseen mishaps, there are guided tours every two years, or when radiation levels permit. The road to the former river confluence is virtually crawling with rock formations, many of which will stun you and knock you out. Near the former townsite of

Tailings, you can still see genuine body-casts from the original accident site. The vibrant (and vibrating) colors of this region will blow your mind! Dress safely!

CAMPING: For the hearty and the previously exposed, a limited number of camping permits are available for a unique and unforgetable stay. However you must notify park rangers, who will notify your next of kin.

Here are a few do's and don't's for the environmentally conscious camper. These safety tips can turn your wilderness experience into one you may survive!

1. PROPER GEAR:
Be sure your clothing is safety approved and bears the DOE-De-Tox label. Is your tent lead-lined? Did you bring a Geiger counter? No-rad sleeping pad?

2. A CLEAN CAMPGROUND:

Gather glowing rocks for light and heat *only*. Never pick them up! If you must move them, use a handy stick or bone. When ready for *lights out* do not attempt to *put them out*. Simply dig a 3,000 foot hole and bury them. In case of campfire meltdown: follow the above procedures, but do them quickly!

3. WILDLIFE: Some remnants of the original wildlife still roam the park, though in mutated forms. Keep a close eye out for the three-eyed badger, the festering bobcat and the desert little-horn. Please, do not pet the animals! It will pull out their remaining clumps of fur.
LEAVE ALL BONES IN PLACE!

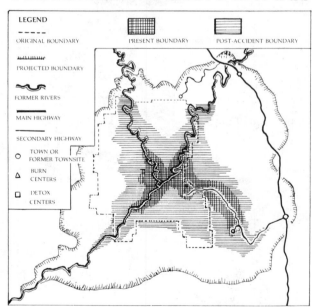

Strontium Coyote

PLUTONIUM NATIONAL PARK

LEGEND
- - - - ORIGINAL BOUNDARY
PRESENT BOUNDARY
POST-ACCIDENT BOUNDARY
.... PROJECTED BOUNDARY
FORMER RIVERS
MAIN HIGHWAY
SECONDARY HIGHWAY
○ TOWN OR FORMER TOWNSITE
△ BURN CENTERS
□ DETOX CENTERS

IT'S YOUR PARK...
NOW LIVE WITH IT!

Plutonium National Park (continued)

EXPLORER: For the intrepid adventurers, with nothing but time on their hands to explore this ever-growing park, "holistic" garments are offered for this unique experience. The ordinary gear of tents, sleeping bags, food, water, etc. are not included as they may not be needed.

Form-fitting fascia

Beeper

Loose-fitting lead-lined tunic

Protective gloves

Hook, line & sinker (pole not necessary)

Anti-rattlesnake knee socks

Multi-soled shoes (see inset)

All-hazard hood

Oxygen tanks and survival manual backpack

Rad counter

Ripcord

Mutant-bite kits (™ trademark reg.)

Radiation reflectors

THE MULTI-SOLE SOLUTION
As the sole of your shoe picks up an unhealthy rad-count, simply rip the bottom-most layer off to expose a new, as yet non-toxic foothold. Sole-boots are available in either 10 or 20 layer models.

EVENING WEAR:
Uni-Sex Faceguard
Mini-porta calray unit
Lead formal wear
Lead hi-heels
Polyester shroud
Oxy-tank pack & survival books
Removable gown and radiation absorbent ground cloth

For the safety conscious day hiker: the LITTLE EGYPT protective shroud.

Side accouterments hold lightweight air purifiers for a small volume nosepiece.

FOR THE R.V. 235 TRAVELLER:

"Port-A-Safe
De-Tox Chambers"

Generator

Waste Cannister

Please place waste
cannister 2,350 feet
underground, prefer-
ably in a salt dome.

NEED TO HANDLE POST-INCIDENT ARTIFACTS?

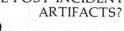

Try the Port-A-Cal ray.

This essential
minaturized unit
is a must when
you "want to keep
your hands to
yourself."

PLUTONIUM NATIONAL PARK

**PEOPLE LEAVE
WITH GLOWING
REPORTS!**

HI THERE! REMEMBER ME? I'm Smoking
the Bear! And I'd feel a whole lot better if
I'd taken the suggestions of Reddy-Kiloton
to heart! The gear shown on these pages
could have saved me from festering, sores,
mange and deep ecology nuts!

So remember folks, only you can pay
close attention or join me in extinction!

Petrified Rock

Most of the nation's National Monuments are built from the materials quarried from this site, where over eons of geologic time the rocks have turned to stone.

Dinosaur National Monument

Bandelo, Utah—Accordion Capital of the World

A statue of Myron Floren dominates Bandelo's public square. Said Mr. Floren, however: "I am not from Bandelo. I have never even heard of Bandelo." This quixotic statement, the subject of many a town meeting, will be put to rest when Myron dies and his remains moved to his beloved Bandelo.

The award-winning (count 'em) Bandelo Marching (and sitting) Accordion Band.

The Utah Map Puzzle

To help keep children and other restless minds occupied while traveling through Utah we have provided a map along with a list of some of Utah's cities, towns and topographical features. To play, just check off the names of the places you have visited, and put a dot on the map at the appropriate place. Those who complete the game can fairly claim to have "seen it all."

PATRIE ARCH
Tarnfeather
Time & Eternity Trailer Park
Sheep Jerky
FLANNEL BOARD FLATS
Rinsin Wash
Yersin Mine
Minibottleneck Canyon
BRUCE CANYON
Gulldarn
Brownbag
Spirit World Amusement Park
BRIGHAM'S KNOB
Hyrum's Crawlspace
Letdown
Geigercounter
Bendover
Alleged Springs
Famine
Gorehead
Rachael David Falls
SNELL'S GROVE
Rankodor
Garmentville
Kantread
Pighump
Bishop's (RV) Court
Not So Green River
Bare Lake
Route 235
Great Salt Lake
Utah Lake

Nogas
Phlemdale
Boxlunch
Alimony
Fallout
Inbred
Marie's Flat
Brane Wash
Dryhump
Vapid City
Breakdown
Meltdown
Chestpain
Pasthope
Thankless
Provo
Sanka Springs
Dream Garden
Wash·Wash

Ocras
Navel
WAH-SKI MOUNTAINS
MT. ELBOW
MT. TINPANALLEY
Salt Lake City
Oohfercute
Oohferneat
Intelligence (ghost town)
No Gas
Grunter
Severe Bumps
PARLEYS NICHE
GAS PASS
Skids
Eyesore
Wallawalla Wash
Bland Canyon
Glowing Debris

Laputa
Thickneck
Wheretheheck
Gingham
BUNKO FLATS
Gypsome
Broken Fanbelt
SONIA'S SINKS
PRIMARY PASS
Lostcow
Dirtycollar
RUDY VALLEY
St. Melvin (Dummar)
Nowearnear
Angstberg
Fealtyville
Tapioca
Vermin
PEDERAST PASS
Smithereens
Joseph's Closet
Luckless
MUTANT SPRINGS
Awgdun
Logie
Lamarr's Elbow
Wet Match
Deseret
Smegma
Curio
Drywell
Dryheave

Promo
Green Liver
Slagheap
WISTFUL VISTA
Steve Canyon
Elaborite Hoax
GNAGY'S DRAW
PUCE CLIFFS
WASH BASIN
Bandelo
Greenlung
Feckless
Trammel
Scintilla
Smallpocks
DONNY'S BROOK
Gerry's Mander
Fallen Arches
Bongo Mtns
Duckburg
Pothole
Decay
Tumorville
Arid
Broken Bottle
Mexican Breath
Banalburg
Bent Needle
BRIGHAM'S BLUFF
Eyestrain
BUNKO FLATS
U AND I MOUNTAINS

The Great Salt Lake

Renowned as the favorite spa of the Utah State Legislature, the Great Salt Lake (or "lake that honks when provoked" as it was known by the Indians) is reclaiming its former territory.

With timely assistance from the Central Utah Project, a nearly complete system of reservoirs, canals and conduits, Utahns fervently hope that Fruit Heights may yet be transformed into the "Venice of the West."

The Great Salt Lake nourishes the brine shrimp, it treats our sewage nicely and insures that unwary tourists never return. Growing rapidly due to a local phenomenon called "heavy runoff," drivers within five miles of the Great Salt Lake are warned under no circumstances to stop their cars and get out to take a look (or leak) at the scenery.

Official Recreation Spot of the Utah Legislature

True Facts of Utah History (Honest!)

THE MORMON TRAIL—The very words suggest rugged pathfinders slashing their way through dense forests and across trackless deserts in their quest to find a route to the Pacific through the Rocky Mountains. Actually, the main body of pioneers followed the Oregon Trail and then the Donner-Reed Trail to within a half mile of present-day Salt Lake City, where they fearlessly trailblazed within four hours the final short, although historic, segment.

"THIS IS THE PLACE"—Having been taken ill on the long trek west, and fallen behind the main body of pioneers, Brigham Young uttered these immortal words from his sick-bed sometime after industrious pioneers had already dedicated the land, begun planting crops and installing irrigation systems.

"NOT ZION"—Early settlers in and around the present-day Zion National Park area named their southern settlement "Little Zion." On a visit to the southern mission Brigham Young told them it was "Not Zion at all." For some time afterwards, the pioneers dutifully called the place "Not Zion." The area was set aside by the federal government in 1909 as Mukuntuweap National Monument. As no one could pronounce the Indian name, President Wilson renamed it Zion National Park nine years later, vindicating the pioneer settlers.

Of related interest, Bryce Canyon National Park was originally called Utah National Monument. Purportedly it was later renamed after its first settler, Ebenezer Bryce, who had commented that "It was one hell of a place to lose a cow."

TIDBITS—

The three main products of Utah's "Cotton Mission" (St. George) were cotton, molasses and wine. The latter industry, although highly successful, was later frowned upon by the church and finally abandoned, because it made the settlers talk funny.

During the "Utah War," the U.S. Army invaded Salt Lake City on June 26, 1857, only to find it silent and abandoned. The Mormons had already fled.

Among Utahns' famous inventions and contributions to world culture are the television and frozen brine shrimp.

94

So Long...

The End

HOWDY PARDNER

Gracing the western periphery of the Salt Flats, the imposing Wendover Cowpoke waves 'Howdy' or 'So long' depending on your point of view. But goodbys are tough so let's say "Howdy pardner. Welcome to Nevada, gateway to California!"

Dearest Voyda,
I did it! Vernal to Wendover walking backwards, and you were right. Nobody noticed. Anyway, I'm just hanging around the Chevron Station having a darkling thought or two.
Yours in good health,
Bork Baker Budge

Distributed by Beagle State Specialties

Voyda Richards Cannon
Smith Young
780 Fortnipple Rd.
Nogas, Utah 84335

Design and layout by Richard Firmage and the authors.
Typesetting by Alphabet Soup.

Cover illustrations by Neil Passey and Mark Knudsen.